THE BEST IS YET TO COME!

Donald Gorbach

ISBN:197618035X
ISBN-13: 978-1976180354

"IF YOU TREAT PEOPLE RIGHT THEY WILL TREAT YOU RIGHT…NINETY PERCENT OF THE TIME."

-FRANKLIN D.ROOSEVELT

Tax Bill

Government Shutdown